Whispers from the Lord

BY JEFF D. ELLIOTT

DORRANCE PUBLISHING CO
EST. 1920
PITTSBURGH, PENNSYLVANIA 15238

Dorrance Publishing Co
585 Alpha Drive
Suite 103
Pittsburgh, PA 15238
Visit our website at *www.dorrancebookstore.com*

ISBN: 979-8-8852-7116-5
eISBN: 979-8-8852-7843-0

Whispers from the Lord

Poet's Profile

Jeff D. Elliott

SAINT HEDWIG, TEXAS

Since childhood, I have loved reading and writing poetry. Most importantly, I believe in the Lord and love him with all my heart and soul. In 1986, I passed away due to suffering with a massive brain tumor. When I passed away, I met with the Lord and told him I was ready to go and please take me. The Lord simply swayed his head no and pointed downward. I quickly returned to earth and felt strapped down in the movement of a vehicle. Waking up in Methodist Hospital in Houston, TX, this was the only memory I had since losing my mind at my home.

I told this experience to my wife, and she said she knew when it happened. She told me while riding in the ambulance, we were just entering the Houston area when the paramedic in the back with me stuck his head up front to the driver and said, "Step on it." She told me she knew he was having trouble keeping me alive. The Lord saved me due to my service of helping others was not complete. I was able to work 20 years as a fire marshal before seizures disabled me. I was able to help many working in the fire service and continue to help others by spreading love and kindness to all those I meet. Then one day, while sitting in my recliner watching TV, the Lord whispered to me, "Go to your desk." At my desk, I asked, "What do you want, Lord?" He whispered, "Write a poem about my mercy." I obeyed his request, and for a little more than a year the Lord whispered to me a subject and sometimes the entire content of the message he wanted poetry written about. I would write down everything he told me, and then transfer his messages into my poetry form. The 100 poems in this book were written by me but came from the word of the Lord that I definitely heard. I Love You, God Bless You, and I pray you will feel the joy of his spirit while reading these poems. Doctors told me many times, "According to your medical records, you should not be alive." I told them, "You have my permission to shred these records, because God is the one that has my medical records and is in total control of every second of life I am blessed with." Again, thank you for reading my poems and I hope you enjoy them.

Contents

God, you are my rock and my king, and I love you with all my heart and soul. Amen.

God's
Blessings

LIVE FOR GOD

God, thank you for your blessings
given throughout each year's season
I pray for those who abuse your gifts
and live their life for selfish reasons

What will it take for these people
to realize how they've been blessed
Praising God with faith and love
knowing God is grading our life's tests

God gives us a life for a reason
a service to follow in a proper way
Normally involving working with others
to spread love and help day by day

True appreciation for life's time
each breath taken is God's gift
I pray for those living only for self
due to life's end they'll be adrift

PRAY BOLDLY

Praying to God is so important
requests for common blessings get old
You must ask for God's blessings indeed
and your blessing requests must be bold

God needs to hear exactly what you want
to better your life and succeed
You can ask God for any type blessing
and also tell him you want them indeed

All you get and all your achievements
are blessings from God of what you want
Pray boldly to God for attention
ask for blessings indeed in a way blunt

When God hears you praying boldly
God will listen and add you to his list
The ones that truly receive his blessings
are those asking for blessing indeed as their wish

GOD SAVING LIFE

Waking in the morning is a blessing from God
giving you a heartbeat and ability to breathe
Answering a prayer for another day with God
knowing his spirit is with you and will never leave

Having Jesus walking by your side
with every step throughout the day
Gives you the feeling of joy for life
praising God and Jesus guides you in this way

God doesn't have only one way of saving
he uses whatever is needed to keep you alive
God's power of knowledge, love, and caring
if it is his want, to put your life back in drive

And all that is required is trust and faith in God
he is always listening and hears every word you say
As a believer, you see, feel, and know this for sure
through God's blessings, he guides you in every way

Saved By God

If you've survived close call with death
probably not just because of doctors' ways
God still has a blessed path for you to follow
reason he blessed doctors with your save

And whatever damage you have suffered
whether due to the surgery or a disease
Don't ever think your life is now over
you can still serve God in a way to please

I am a victim of a massive brain tumor
my recovery was said they did not know it
But living on for God's blessed saving
20 years as firefighter and now a poet

No matter what your outcome may be
God provides strength through all seasons
Remember your experience of being saved
convincing others God's love is the reason

This may be the path God wants you to follow
helping others to bring him into their hearts
Because so many have to see true results
before faith and belief in God can start

God's Goals Given

Freedom given for choice of goals
use knowledge realistic not odd
For help obtaining what you choose
live a life of serving our God

No matter what type of goals
work, lifestyles, or body health
We all need aid throughout our life
amazing blessings from God are wealth

When choosing God as your leader
you'll find serving him is not a chore
Results of feeling strength of love
walking with Jesus through open doors

A life with comfort in your heart
giving to others this love and care
Will bless your living until time of death
and guide you to heaven up God's stairs

A Brother

Being blessed with a brother
relationship based on love and care
One you can always depend upon
to be a part of your life, as an equal share

Times of communication so important
whether in person or on the phone
Knowing all that's said is in trust
and words spoken, true to the bone

Brother, a one you can call on
when you need those times to vent
Only person that will listen and support
with no limits on needed time spent

The bond you share with a brother
a type of security that is so true
Knowledge of each other's business
always kept between you two

Brother, a special gift from God
a person in life, unlike any other
Yet, brought into life just like all
by God, and a father and mother

Most brothers are related by blood
but truly and certainly don't have to be
A man, dedicating life, love, and care to another
a blessing from God, a brother given to thee

ALL ARE PREACHERS

We all can say we are preachers
whatever the subject may be
But mainly God wants his word spoken
wanting this subject preached by thee

Yes, we all have our main topics
we love teaching others about
But just remember so often the times
God wants us talking about his route

So also talk about your blessings
the reason you achieved your success
Then start speaking those words about God
being a preacher talking more than less

You'll soon find others love to hear
praising God for a life being so strong
And then they'll start preaching back
Turning church service from short to long

Praying to God

Showing love for God is so important
but praying to God is act number one
If you want to receive blessings in life
telling God what you want has to be done

Truly being a Christian and serving God
all basics for life will come your way
But to reach your great destiny in life
God needs to hear surely what you pray

God wants us to make own decisions
in ways to help ourselves and others too
God must indeed hear our requests for blessings
to know what types are needed for you

Imagine the number of prayers God hears daily
God's listening to prayers does not ever get old
But to get best results from praying to God
ask for blessings indeed and speak them bold

BLESSINGS

What is this belief in blessings
we control how much we get
Just work hard and watch your back
so during life you don't get bit

Living only for self is not what
God intended for you only to do
If faith and love for God is missing
your gift of life may soon be through

If you are living life with success
you better feel you've been blessed
Thanking God for all you have been given
realizing the way you live is God's test

So think about when your life ends
did you thank God for blessings or not
Truly then you will see your life's destiny
from heaven above or a place that's hot

All goodness comes from God's blessings
his mercy and love blessing us each day
Belief, praise, and love given to God
results in blessings to come in a right way

Blessing Clock

When we pray to God for help
God quickly prepares help his way
People's fault is their impatience
expecting help to come that very day

Blessings are given at God's discretion
don't feel like you're placed on dock
God knows times of need and deserve
and controls his blessing clock

Don't doubt God's hearing calls for help
show him you're also working to solve
Just sitting back expecting God to do all
might cause a halt for blessing to evolve

Most all need to pray for God's help
keep love and faith for God to cure
God knows what we need before we ask
his blessing clock is always ticking for sure

HAVE PATIENCE

There are so many times in life
wondering when blessings will come our way
God always has our blessings prepared
delivery time may be years, months, or days

Keep your patience and trust in God
don't feel stuck in place where you are
Or frustrated you're not being treated right
with God in heart you'll stay up to par

God is just waiting for you to be ready
so blessings are handled in the right way
Stay on God's path with strong confidence
and blessings will come on a special day

When your blessings show up and happen
you'll understand why you had to wait
Because blessings will change life abundantly
and praise God for being in charge of your fate

World Without God Leading

A world breeding destruction
taking of lives as main goal
Turning faith to one named Satan
and falling into inferno's hole

Why this change of direction
who wins when evil rules
Fighting one against the other
acting along with Satan as fools

The cause being very plain and simple
removing God's presence from earth
Man and evilness now the leader
slapping God's face for our birth

No more God-loving righteous leaders
destroying youthful devotion to earth
Actions taken without care for others
God's gift of emotion has no worth

There is no person here on earth
who has correction in great abound
So therefore worldwide devastation
cannot by people be turned around

Only one cure for this evilness
praise and faith in God, to return and lead
Bringing love, truthfulness, and caring back
and replanting life with God's holy seed
When God sees us walking back on his path
blessed strength and guidance will prevail
Removing sin and Satan as leader
pushing all evilness back into hell

Gifts From God

GIFTS FROM GOD

God knows the number of hairs on your head
yet some ask does God hear my prayers
Never question the attention that God gives
to all our needs, he is always aware

God gives you needed wisdom
a friend that is always there
We all are children of God
given a full life with none to spare

Your faith in God makes him happy
he loves our willingness to give trust
God sends blessings to affirm our faith
and eases our burdens, so we won't bust

God removes our transgressions from us
turn away from your sins and head east
Never turning around to head back west
and God will forgive, with mercy and peace

GOD OUR CREATOR

God is the creator of all
from birds to people like you and me
God knowing everything about us
and so caring about how our lives will be

True faith to God opens his door
all prayers from you will be heard
God is always listening to us
his door is always open, hearing all our words

God is the source of our wisdom
asking for it in faith, you will receive
Having trust in God to give you wisdom
your answers will come, wait and see

God is always with us in life
no matter what you're doing, or where you are
God, a friend who always has the time
to listen and give counsel, whatever it is for

God wants to adopt you as his own child
a life in God's kingdom, truly worth living
Ones on earth portraying life, out of touch and drab
truth is, living with light and life of heaven is never ending

PROTECTION THROUGH FAITH

Being weary and carrying heavy burdens
turn your life to God, and he will give you rest
He knows our strength and amount it will tolerate
to provide you ease, wearing God's burden yoke is best

Your faith in God, is what will make him glad
you must seek God and believe he does exist
And live in a trusting relationship with him
God will send blessings, helping you with life's risks

God looks after us with gentle, watchful love
a tender-hearted guardian, one who gives us care
And in his mercy, doesn't revisit what he has forgiven
faith in God removes, life's dangers speaking beware

God's protection will surround your life on all sides
his angels fighting the devil and all of his evil plans
When certain bad things happen, don't think the angels failed
God is doing something else, to place protection in your hands

HEAR HIS VOICE

God is the creator of knowledge
an energy source we cannot see
But blessed with this in many ways
God gives words of poetry to me

Just like this one I'm writing now
God placed in my mind these words
I just go sit and write them down
a poem is formed from what I heard

Many times it's just a subject
sometimes entire message is sent
Letting me place them in poetry form
if message is truly what God meant

I speak to God throughout each day
the power of his voice is sent back
God's message so clear when you listen
he'll guide you clearly without lack

I praise God for every poem written
guiding my pencil as I write again
His message today is for all to listen
to be guided righteously, Amen

Helping Others

Gift of help to others is serving God as well
no one is capable of performing all life's skills
Mechanics, plumbing, and electrical to name a few
always helping others, accepting payment of their thrill

Many times in life, you'll find ones in need
helping them causes friendship, or you are their fan
And this showing of love and care for others
will tell you why God put a skill in your hand

If you live life, without having care for helping others
and only using your talents as a profit gain for you
The loss of love, respect, and friendship in life
and facing hardships in your life without blessings is true

God knows all aspects pertaining to our life and thoughts
and God's mercy given to us, proof helping others is right
So whenever you see people facing troubles without help
show them your love and caring, putting help in their sight

A time in your life will come when you will require help
living with God in your life, help will come for you
Knowing the love and caring help you've given others in the past
is why help comes to you so quickly, with a blessing as your clue

GIFT OF COMMON SENSE

An outside kinda fellow
labor is what he loves
Whatever type of work it is
he jumps on it with a shove

These guys are hard to find
and so lucky if you do
Cuz helping you with a chore
easy for them as tying a shoe

Some thinking they're not smart
but oh, they are so wrong
Without these gifted fellas
living with breakages would be the song

Most of what they have in brain
form of knowledge not taught in school
Known as God's gift of common sense
for items built and repaired, they are rule

And for those that always are bragging
about everything that they've done
However when facing work causing sweat
these are the ones that turn tail and run

Luckily I know a man with these skills
sometimes saying, I'm not real smart
Wrong, because if he asked me for a fixin'
the result would be, this item broken apart

CHOICE OF LIFE

Living with God in your life
is like fueling your car to drive
Both such an easy task to achieve
yet only one lasts forever with strive

We devote most time to personal things
thinking we are in control of it all
But without your love and faith in God
one day, problems will give you a hard fall

When God is taken in with love and truth
he will always be watching over your life
And when you are in need of his help
God will solve problems without any strife

So think hard and make the right choice
living with comfort, protection, and love
Because if you choose a life on your own
when life ends, you may miss heaven above

True Happiness

A poem to promote happiness
without feelings of depression or hate
Believe in God, with love and trust
and prayer will open the happiness gate

There are many good people on earth
walk with them, happily making a friend
Our time on earth is really not long
and life should be happy, enjoyed until end

Hope for success is still a great quest
some blessed with this being in their reach
Making money, fun times and happiness
don't give up on success, making life a breach

Keeping God and Jesus in your life
walking in the footprints to guide you
Causing happiness on earth as your path
leading to everlasting life in heaven so true

Enjoy Your Life

Enjoy each day of this life
that you have been so granted
Another day of growth for you
from life's seed God planted

Keep happiness as your leader
and spread God's gift of love
God wants to witness the goodness
he blessed you with from above

Meet life's challenges head on
always pushing aside defeat
Having God in heart as your leader
you'll not be swept off your feet

Every day of life we're given
praise God with all your heart
Time of living within God's hands
enjoyment will abound until you part

TALENT

God blesses us all with talents
some easy and some hard
It doesn't matter what yours is
talent is truly a blessed reward

My brain damaged by huge tumor
and the surgery too for sure
I did not think retaining knowledge
would be included with my cure

Believe me, my doctors were fantastic
but God was in charge of outcome
Keeping my thoughts to write in brain
due to my poetry about him not done

So God's blessings continue each day
my given talent of being able to write
God constantly putting words in my brain
proving the tumor did not win the fight

Whatever talent you are blessed with
use it to keep your life in drive
God-given talent definitely a benefit
so don't ever push it off to the side

MANY SKILLS GIVEN

If God has blessed you with a talent
whatever this skill will be
Don't ignore and let it pass you by
God's blessings are given for a need

For example, if it is poetry
and you've received the gift of rhyme
Start writing with thought for the words
surprisingly a poem will occur in mind

Maybe it is the gift of art
drawing and painting with color
Creating your designs so unique
to amaze and show beauty to others

Might be the skills of a handyman
able to do repairs of all types
Including the art of constructing
from furniture to a child's kite

Never let God's blessings, pass by unnoticed
always giving praise and thanks from you
Definition of his blessings are unlimited
and could be something God wants you to do

Mindful Writing

If you have some paper and pencil
And also have the ability to write
The words written down from thoughts
could guide you and others just right

Let your thoughts be the guide
a subject will be chosen fast
Keep writing all words in sentences
amazing how long it will last

You may think, just my story of life
yet there's a reason for writing it down
Your story may be helpful to others
and God may want it spread around

So, don't waste time just thinking
without putting these thoughts on paper
This may be the path God wants you to travel
giving your life a blessed forward caper

New paths are given throughout your life
never think you're unable to follow due to age
If God puts this path to follow in your mind
you have true given strength to go this way

Future Success

Moving life forward towards success
your faith in God must be real
And by keeping past failures a part of life
for God's help not a right way to deal

Yes, God will always hear you talk
but is God listening the true key
Your past failures have been forgiven
show God a righteous new way from thee

To definitely turn life around to move on
have faith in God's teachings as true
Quit requesting forgiveness of past failures
start asking God for help in renewing you

You'll begin to feel and see blessings come
and success will be moving within your reach
God will now listen to all what you need
when you have disconnected past failures' leash

THANKSGIVING?

A day with the title of Thanksgiving
a day off from work called holiday
A meeting with family to share a meal
talking about Christmas and forgetting to pray

So enjoy an abundance amount of food
then sit back into chair to watch football game
What does this holiday Thanksgiving really mean
a day eating with family that has a special name

Reality is every meal eaten, every single day
for every meal, thanks should be given to God by you
Don't think, once a year, thanks to God is enough
proving you're not living with God in life, this being the clue

Praise God for all you have each and every day
from the time of waking up, till the time of going to bed
God always watching over us, knowing the life we live
if you do not believe this, you're offering life to evil instead

God gives us love, joy, and happiness to live life with him
if you don't feel his presence at home, he is not there
Remove depression and heaviness from the life you are in
by bringing God and Jesus into life, Devil sent elsewhere

Again Thanksgiving should be celebrated each and every day
prayers and praise to God, showing faith and trust your giving
God's presence will then shine a bright light upon you and your life
and you will see, feel, and enjoy his blessings, God's gift to the living

Careful Trust in Others

When trying to improve your life
working under another's command
For some reason it never seems
that the money ends up in your hand

Putting your trust in what they say
following all orders and advice
The result of success falls back in time
hearing from them, times coming are nice

They love to talk of their success
and how you can achieve this too
Yet it always seems you have to invest
your money to stay in their groove

They love you as part of a family
praising God for all money taken in
But how long for you to see this
years and years of devotion to win

I say the way to improve your life
is by praising God, and following his way
Having trust in him to take care of you
until he calls, to enter heaven on the last day

Joyful Living

Enjoyment is a time to strive for
joy, a feeling that can't be beat
And when these two join together
blessings of great times are at your feet

A time of life we ourselves create
by living positive and with love
Keeping life's negatives in their place
accepting good times from God above

Times of fun children forever promote
yearning for all to follow along
Their first learning is living for joy
not ever wanting to feel it has gone

Whatever life's times will deal us
never let the bad into your heart
Our unlimited love for enjoyment
is what keeps us from falling apart

God and Family

Born into this world with family
you'll have a mom and dad
And most of the time some siblings
to share all life, good and bad

A family is your first teacher
at home and throughout school
And also taught about religion
always obeying the family rules

At first you're always guided
so you know which way to go
But later on choices are made
knowledge improving as you grow

All family forever being there
to support you on your way
With decisions about your life
you'll have to make day by day

Because that day will finally come
working to achieve your goals
And with God and family as your leaders
you'll make the right choice for your role

Yes, family is so important
but God placed you here on earth
So keep love in your heart for both
to enjoy and truly know your worth

PATH TO DESTINY

We all are given a destiny for life
known by God before our birth
And by keeping God in our heart
you'll reach that destiny here on earth

Don't try and be your only guide
or let others determine your fate
Follow God's path with your heart
guiding you through his open gates

Dreams are real and can come true
God's destiny for you stays laid out
Praise and love for God is start
to stay on path of your destiny's route

Negative ways can knock you back
so stay positive with trust in your Lord
God protects you from a tripping gait
stay strong and he'll walk you on board

God and
His Son, Jesus

God and Jesus Are One

I live with God and Jesus in my life
serving them in the way they want to see
The feelings of love from both of them
exceed what any emotions felt can be

Jesus is always walking closely by my side
twenty-four hours each day
And I speak with him so constantly
hearing exactly what we both will say

Like most, I've had many problems
issues involving money and health
God always has stepped in and saved me
providing a security greater than wealth

Having God and Jesus so close
feelings of love, faith, and truth are clear
And no worry about any of your needs
they help you with all, treating you as their dear

Feelings while praying and asking of them
is in no way like talking without reason
God hears and knows everything you want and need
and will bless you with his loving season

For all, please praise and serve our God
and have Jesus walking by your side
Feeling all the love and joy of life
following Jesus as your guide

BELIEVE IN GOD

God shows himself, with blessings and his love
some say if they cannot see him, they cannot believe
Devil shows himself with depression and evil acts
and without belief in God the devil will be your lead

God delivers you into world, blessed with his love
raised with God's love, and taught to follow his path
Yet when you age and grow, your decisions can be changed
and sadly, one can push God aside and live life with wrath

I pray every day for those who do not believe in God
and do not walk in Jesus' footprints guiding you through life
Because living without God and having devil by your side
will give your life filled with struggles and with strife

I pray one day you will see the beaming light from God
and feel the spirit of Jesus walking by your side
A life believing in God with faith, love, and trust
will keep your footprints in the path and Jesus as your guide

OUR ROCK AND KING

Bigger than the world, is our loving God
do not conform to the world, for renewal of your mind
Acceptable and perfect, keep in mind Godly groove
with God as our ally, adversity cannot control our time

People's needs, drives, and desires have not changed
bible contents address this as no other writings on earth
Walk in Jesus' footsteps, sharing with others our kind of love
God's gift that is still with us, one received at our birth

Gospel is good news, Jesus a savior who is now our Lord
power of God for salvation to everyone who has faith
Setting the mind on the Spirit is a goal of life and peace
God searches our hearts and minds, prayers delivering us his grace

These times will always come, as if we have messed up life
but God, in business of redemption will give us that needed rouse
Transforming unlivable, thoughtless space into lovely habitation
utmost belief you keep, there is always hope when God is in house

Pain, frustration, sorrow, disappointment, and depression
living in a fallen world, not wanting to give God praise
But during tough times, still thank God for what is right
praising God continually, our life and mind will begin to raise

BECOMING A CHRISTIAN

Devoting your heart and soul to God
walking with Jesus by your side
The spreading of your love to all others
is your beginning of the Christian ride

Not something that can only be done once
you must follow God's teachings day after day
And lessening your commitment of sins
will continue your life in a Christian way

Totally devoting your life to be a Christian
requires always living with God in your heart
Spreading God's love is your main chore
to keeping good and evilness far apart

Realizing it is the life you have genuinely wanted
showing your love and faith so true
Keeping God's blessings flowing your way
knowing you have opened the gate to heaven too

God will provide your leadership
being a Christian following his path
Blessed with joy and love on earth forever
without your life being cursed with wrath

Our God

God, our creator of heaven and earth
God, what has happened to those given birth
God, why have so many turned away
God, not followers and praising life's worth

God, you are always our true ruler and leader
God, our lives begin with love to serve you
God, who are so many now looking for to lead
God, and due to their search have become so rude

God, aren't they truly aware of the devil's presence
God, why don't they feel the evilness of this type of follow
God, you have taught us about the life in hell
God, help us to deter those choosing such a hollow

God, from beginning teaching us love is to live by
God, we know to spread love to enemies and all
God, having faith, praise, and love for you as our path
God, and with this you give heaven at end as our call

God, we are praying for your help to change life
God, you are our only cure as our Father from birth
God, we feel your presence and know you will not leave
God, thank you and please remove evilness from earth

God, as Christians, we love you with all heart and soul
God, we pray all others will see the light of your love
God, help them to put you back in their lives and heart
God, please show all the kingdom, power, and glory from above

WALKING WITH JESUS

Living with Jesus by your side
gives you life, sturdy as stone
And whatever situation comes to you
you will never be facing it alone

The feeling of Jesus walking with you
making the footprints for you to follow
Will guide you in the right direction
without worry of falling into a hollow

You will also feel the true joy of life
being with Jesus, family, and friends
Often praise Jesus and walk in his footprints
and your joy for life will never end

Jesus is our given leader to follow
the reason God has him here on earth
And living with God and Jesus in your life
is what will give your time here a worth

Joy With Jesus

Happiness is the birth of joy
a feeling we all desire and want
Walk with Jesus by your side
he will lead you on this hunt

Jesus blesses our life with a path
one guiding us with joy
Knowing our feelings when reaching a goal
like a little boy with his first toy

Now if you sway and falter
sidestepping and leaving his path
You will not be judged and cursed
to lose your goals and feel wrath

Praise Jesus and raise your hand
he will pull you back on course
Give all faith and trust to Jesus
feeling and loving his guidance force

Now walk with Jesus hand in hand
following his footsteps on your path laid out
You'll feel path widen with eruption of joy
and all goals will be reached on your life's route

God's Love

GOD'S MERCY

Definition of mercy means one doesn't deserve kind treatment
but God's mercy follows us every day and every night
Asking God for mercy and forgiveness for our daily sins
erases our chalkboard of misdeeds, starting our next day right

God's mercy is given for everyone's behavior
his love and caring flowing out to all human forms
Don't believe the bad ones should receive God's harsh judgment
God our Lord is gracious and merciful, not a resort for harm

God's request is for all of us to be merciful
loving your enemies, proving your children of the Lord
God does not approve of enemy attitudes and actions
but giving mercy instead of meanness, is rightly, yet hard

God does not remember our sins, only his great love for us
we are loved and saved, as children of his own
God's mercy makes everything good, and we owe him our lives
thank and bless him forever, his love allows us to be grown

Project mercy for all, including the weak and weary
those ones with relational struggles, illness, and grief
Keeping yourself in the love of God, and the mercy of our Lord
believers can help these folks, showing God's mercy gives relief

Choosing mercy is a Victory, shown to our loving God
promoting yourself as merciful, not as a self-righteous one
Actions keeping God's love and blessings, flowing into your life
God will love you as a follower, like Jesus, God's loving son

THE LORD'S PRAYER

Our Father who art in heaven
hallowed be thy name
A name all should have in their heart
our God, one carrying the most fame

Thy Kingdom comes
thy will be done
We shall live to serve God
the one carrying all our funds

On earth as it is in heaven
give us this day our daily bread
God provides us all our needs
living and after life is dead

And forgive us of our trespasses
as we forgive those who trespass against us
A life lived, avoiding commitment of sins
and not living with a want or need of lust

And lead us not into temptation
but deliver us from evil
God doesn't entice us to unwise ways
truly all his guidance is legal

For thine is the kingdom and the power
and the glory for all, Amen
A prayer for God, spoken in the best way
always our loving leader, for women and men

Love Sonnet

Love, endearing gift from God received by all for the
Quest of Christianity and a path of entry into heaven

Love gives the true joy of walking with and helping others

Love is built with solidity, but yet it can be broken

Love meant for ways of goodness, but some use for abuse and advantage

Love, created by God who gave it the start, and made love everlasting

Love has no fenced-in boundaries so growth of love is unlimited

Love can be altered by others through evil thoughts or uses

Love for Mother and family teaches your soul what it's for

Love giving trust and faith for a special one we name as a friend

Love, so enticing just for one, never wanting it to leave your heart and
stay with you through life

Love, joining another for lifetime, confessing promises to God of care and
protection with an unending growth of love

Love, creating God's children to enter his world and proving you are
sharing his gift of life

Love, life's main goal to live for, creating joy and happiness for all of
those you touch

Love, praising God for all his blessings and each day of your life, and
remember the limits of love because it will not die with one's passing

MARRIAGE

Devoting one's entire life to another for love
honoring, cherishing, and oh, so much more
And making these promises to another before God
is saying I Love You, and accept all the chores

Not stating that it's wrong, I believe in love totally
and I've honored my chores for all our years
I just want people to know, before saying I Do
it's more than a ring and words, I love you so much, dear

Life as one and life as two, will show lifetime differences
such as all you do, no longer a one person's choice
After this connection of two, love reveals all its factors
both learn very quickly, love carries another one's voice

Oh, yes, you have to listen to much at very many times
your opinions and your wants are no longer one-sided
And if both don't honor each other's voiced thoughts
They'll experience love and life can really become collided

Before this commitment, make sure you both totally know
what each of you have been carrying in life's carriage
And included with your love, an ultimate friendship exists
To give and receive joy and love, with your choice of marriage

STRENGTH OF LOVE

If you are a true believer
love in heart for God above
Life will be filled with blessings
with best one being God's love

The spreading of your love
used properly as a cure
Guiding and helping others
with God-given love so pure

Love is God's main purpose
for placing you here on earth
To show and give love to all
sharing his love given to you at birth

Yes, love is the easy answer
for all people getting along
And using love together to solve problems
using God's gift of love to stay strong

Love and Faith

Jesus is the portrait of true love that never ends
we are called to show equalness with the faithful love of God
The three pillars of life are faith, hope, and greatness of love
love is more important than getting stuff done or doing a great job

God's dealing with humans is by a strand of undying love
weaved into the hearts of children, to carry love across world for all
Love not only in word or speech, better shown in truth and action
selfless love, giving kindness and help for others, preventing them to fall

Love through actions verifies who we are as Christians
Jesus, supreme example, by entering our reality on earth
Experiencing temptation and lifted our burden by enduring the cross
eternal life given by rising again, and a promise to return proving his worth

Love is essential, owing love to one another or having nothing in life
creating joy for personal sacrifice, giving kindness and help to others
A path of patience is walking on the high road of love
dole love, patience, and kindness to strangers as they are brothers

Love is not boastful, rude, or rejoicing in wrongdoings
and does not insist on its own way, irritable or resentful
So think about your recent actions, words, and attitudes
it will let you know if behaving as God wants, love as truthful

God and Jesus, our leaders and ones who are what truth means
knowing love is tough, but the choice is always worthwhile
Ones choosing to go their own way, pray for their safe return to God
and keep love kind and true, with marriage and raising a child

Believe in Jesus Christ and provide love for one another
having Jesus in your life goes hand in hand just like faith and love
Jesus fills us with his love, and flowing his love through us, proves our faith
so show and give authentic love, verifying faith to God above

LOVE NEVER DIES

When God calls a helpful person
for their time to move along
The goodness this one started
is meant for another to carry it on

You need not to be a hero
or one rolling in high wealth
To continue the act of helping
providing others love and health

All of us are God's children
our time of passing his call
But does not mean his choice
should stop love and help for all

Some are missed more than others
blessed with goodness to spread
God gives this blessing to many
so acts of love don't die when dead

COPING WITH ENEMIES

Through life you will meet many
People that are good, and some bad
Live with God's love in proper way
and cause both types to become glad

Now the good ones are the easiest
to get along with and make friends
Putting fun and help in front
hopefully keeping without an end

Now the bad ones show up too
some wanting to be your enemy
But treating them the same as good
is God's way to make them leave

An enemy wants to cause anger
to bring you down to their level
If you fall for their evil tricks
you'll be playing a game with the devil

Treating an enemy with God's love
will make an evil mind confused
And eventually will make them feel sorry
for causing God's love to be so abused

God's love cannot be defeated
a gift from heart given to all of us
The true and proper tool to use
making evilness feel its lush

PEACE?

What now is this word called peace
and where does it exist on earth
Defined as a sense of calmness
but in this world now has no worth

If living in an area without war
taking of another's life is a sin
Yet in all countries that are fighting
killing is righteousness for a win

I believe peace is what God desires
by spreading love from one to another
So why has hatred become the ruler
dripping red blood the enticing color

All should pray for peace to return
and start acting in a way to cause this
Imagine a world with peace spread all over
living with each other in total bliss

My Father

A quiet man, limits on speaking
very giving with joyful times of fun
His devotion, care, and love for family
expressed in special ways by this one

An unfortunate inherited temper
mostly controlled, a number of times not
Father's main goal, strong family structure
a constant securing of the family knot

Always there for all of us
a life of constant routine
Never showing himself as better
always showing and giving esteem

Problem, not living the way he wanted
showing wife true faith and love
Not retiring on time, and sneaky with smoking
death calling him quickly, from God above

A man I truly respect, love, and miss
though in heaven, still feel his spirit near me
Living with God's decision, still regretting my loss
blessed with my loving Father, providing a life without need

WASTED EMOTIONS

Loving people because their stars
placed high in our dreams and trust
Knowing a star we strive to be like
and respecting their values as a must

Dress and good looking way above all
living in mansions built so fine
Judgment of them as a purity
like the sipping of a fine wine

These stars are just people like you
for wrong reasons we've chosen to adore
Although their lives give out a calling
don't wait for their hand to knock on your door

Remember that when true love is given
to a star or idol just playing a part
This is truly wrong, and a waste of love
given by God, who placed true love in our hearts

Problems We All Face

THE DEVIL

The fallen angel and leader of evilness
having love for hate and destruction
Non-believers in God are his targets
to obtain and guide in his direction

Searching for those with confusion
living life, not knowing right from wrong
These people will be devil's students
taught to walk with him and be strong

Devil's strength of evilness is overbearing
making it easy to harm and kill others
Rewarding his followers with life in hell
and treating them as sisters and brothers

Love for damage of free-burning fire
one lesson from the devil you'll learn
Because when you're dropped in pit of hell
devil laughs with pleasure, watching you burn

There is only one way to keep devil afar
having Jesus walking by your side
Living life with love and helping others
with faith and trust in God as your only guide

A Failing Country

Our country and our land are in a horrible condition
with hatred, lack of love, and elimination of God
Once a country yearned for from people across the world
now disrespected and weak with most conditions beyond odd

People named politicians, took leadership in hand
removing God from structures and procedures of life
Allowing evilness to move in and start taking control of all paths
causing faith, love, and praise to God unable to be suffice

We continue to allow the hardships steadily to grow worse
with political leaders squandering our money and ways
Deleting our ability to live well and destroying military protection
people without God in heart, accepting their lies day by day

Our children mostly suffer, no pleasing future in their sight
and parental raising is pitiful without discipline, respect, and faith
Children now thinking of death and violence as a way to play
no love for God, fear of sin, and unable to show others grace

There is but only one solution, for making country great again
removal of the evilness, by the power of God's will
People coming back together with God, giving love and help to all
placing love and religion back in our lives, God, country's leader, the deal

Our World Now

We are all living in a world now
so far, far away from the best
Expanding with fight and hatred
with brink of war causing us stress

And what have we done with religion
people and churches going own ways
Choosing own interpretations to live by
and pushing God's teachings out to bay

How come are we living so apart from others
acts of love and help have become just words
Everyone thinking just for themselves
God and others in life, separated with curb

Maybe someday our ways will change back
but in the near future, not seen at all
Only faith and love for God and others
will put cracks needed in this evilness wall

Dealing With Evilness

God is the one who placed us here
we ask why in a place so hard to cope
To show God how we strive to spread his love
and with Jesus in life there is true hope

To live through evilness here on earth
stay on God's path with Jesus by side
Be positive and always pray each day
and your blessings and destiny will abide

Yes, life on earth is a difficult test
but with God one we all can pass
By keeping faith, praise, and love in heart
you'll evade evilness and goodness will last

God gave you blessing of life through birth
and God is the one that will take life back
But while living on earth don't let evilness
show God your love or trust in him was lack

Life's Long Road

Life's long road to travel
thinking you lack the needed time
Only way to reach your destiny
keeping your travel on God's line

People, things causing you problems
creating a dire travel delay
Don't let problems stop you in track
prevail and keep moving your way

We know not how much time is needed
to reach the destiny on our life's road
Truly the reason to stay on God's path
knowing interpretation of your life's code

So many don't reach their true destiny
wasting so much time going own ways
Keeping faith and love for God in heart
guides your travel quickly day by day

STEPPING STONES

Past is a set of stepping stones
a source of growth for our minds
Showing difference of good and bad
teaching us not to slip and fall behind

Using your past as a benefit
not as a crutch for slack
Reason for going forward on stepping stones
prevention of life from falling back

Learning is a required process
to find and know right from wrong
Using them properly as guides
keeps life steady and helps you along

Many fail making wrong decisions
a huge pushback for them in life
Knowing what is right, stop and leap forward
don't let mistakes cause you strife

The choice of right decisions
should never be taken for granted
Use them for keeping life in line
keeping feet on stepping stones well planted

Everyone is given a path to follow
staying on stepping stones provides you ease
Remembering the times of slips and falls
but now back on path, giving you please

Time in Church

Churches are truly a special place
to show faith and love for God
Normally open on a day called Sunday
to bless rest of week not being at odds

Think about your feelings when at church
being humble and kind to all around
Praising God for all of your blessings
presence of God's love is abound

Attending a church is a great routine
to feel and learn God's message of love
But don't think like many this one hour a week
guarantees you a sure entry to heaven above

A church service should definitely remind us
who we should be living each day of life for
Our God spreading his gift of love and mercy
every day to all others whether near or far

TRUE BELIEF

Belief is trust and confidence
in a principal or opinion
And believing is accepting this
as a true and real conviction

Sometimes one uses a belief
to gather others into their trust
And then is able to control their faith
for the benefits of their own lust

Before you commit to a belief
be sure it's true and real
Conviction and believing of just what is heard
can be making a lifelong demoniac deal

That's why belief in our God
is a proven truthful commitment
And keep Jesus by your side for protection
from those whose beliefs are rueful

When belief in God and Jesus is truthful
and for them, your life is served
Ne'er trust in those who abuse beliefs
Causing you to lose God's course and swerve

WALKING ALONE

How many of you are out there
walking through your life alone
Depending on luck for good to come
your cries for help only heard on phones

You people are truly the ones we pray for
knowing how trying and scary life can be
Alone not having a true source of protection
and traveling life's path your soul can't see

Open your soul and heart to God
bringing in Jesus to walk by your side
And you will no longer be walking alone
your protection and guidance will abide

You will hear and feel the presence
of Jesus, flowing his love through your heart
And walking alone will vanish forever
life given to God does not fall apart

Praying please put your faith in our Lord
and then help others to see God's light
Because by walking alone in life
you'll never be guided in a way right

MISSING A FRIEND

Losing that special personal touch
with the one you've known so long
A separation of a friendship for years
a life experience so hard and wrong

Knowing lifestyle choices will differ
causing changes and moves occurring in time
But losing a friend from sight and touch
is like being the victim of a crime

At least ways are available
to stay in a type of touch
Using a phone for talking or texting
but without personal touch, it isn't enough

Praise God for knowing importance
of friendship with love in heart
The blessing will eventually come
where you are no longer far apart

The thought of seeing and hugging
your friend so missed, again
Proves faith in God and praying
doesn't create losses, but gives you a win

Making a Decision

A decision should not be a problem
a chore all often have to do
Stay calm and answers will develop
or request help from others for you

All decisions are not deemed final
changes do not state confusion
Times thinking of something better
causing a much more practical solution

When anger enters time of decisions
be smart and post a delay
Making decisions without calmness
will cause wrong choices that day

Decisions are truly a test
of the way we control our acts
Using our intelligence properly
moving life forward instead of back

HARD TIMES

Life's challenges are so often hard,
creating a time named depression
Defeating these times is a test
to show you've learned God's lessons

Bad times are usually developed
by evil forces floating around
Facing them with God by your side
will give you strength to knock them down

These hard times always come and go
never seeming to reach an end
But living with God in your heart
you always will be the one to win

Don't think you're dealt more than others
they're a down time we all must face
But by being a truly blessed Christian
hardships cannot stop your life's pace

DEALING WITH TROUBLES

We all live through times of trouble
up until the time called to die
Praying to God that these troubles
are not the result of a sinful lie

Reasons for trouble can be confusing
causing stress and you to get mad
Control and concentration on solutions
will make troubles not seem as bad

All your troubles are not created by you
troubles have an unlimited source
But so many times they fall on your back
making you walk the correction course

Yes, troubles do have to be dealt with
just don't let them get the best of you
Stay true, praise God, and help will come
giving you the win and troubles will lose

DEFEATING BAD TIMES

When scams in life come your way
don't get depressed or feel down
Ask God boldly to remove them from you
looking towards blessings that are abound

Constant prayer to God is your defense
to keep negatives astray in your life
Ask God to keep blessing you indeed
and eliminate stress to family and wife

When you place your heart in God's hands
God will push you through bad towards good
And keep praying for what you truly want
all God's blessings will come as they should

Never look towards others as controlling your life
God is the one that holds your life's folder
And God will allow you to reach your destiny
by serving him properly and praying bolder

PROBLEM COPING

When you give God life's control
and have Jesus by your side
Your progress cannot be set back
move forward with faith and pride

Problems always try to get
in the way, just small bumps along the road
Dodge and run over them sturdy
or leap the bumps like a toad

When serving God as he wants
and blessed with signs of success
Remember God is the one leading
so no reason for problem stress

Yes, others' faults can seem difficult
not yours so face them with ease
There's only one in charge of destiny
God, and for you he'll give please

DEPENDING UPON OTHERS

Take control of life given to you
from your Father, God above
Not letting others guide your way
and removing obstacles with a shove

God has blessed you with the ability
to pick and choose your own path
But living with God's strength of love
will defeat all attempts on you of wrath

The leading ones will always succeed
and help others to follow their way
Depending on others for gift to lead
is a waste of time spent every day

God is our leader we depend upon
knowing our purpose in life from birth
Don't waste efforts depending upon others
keep control of your life to always rank first

Living with Disability

Whatever disability you have
lack of body parts or brain
Praise God and keep on living
even though disabilities are so lame

Keep pushing and competing
to strengthen your body and mind
This positive way of living
will defeat disability in time

Disability did not kill you
just set you back in a bad way
Knowing survival was God's blessing
and he has want and reasons for you to stay

Disabilities can be used to help others
realizing how blessed with health they are
And hopefully give prayer for your recovery
along with God's blessings, your life can go far

Don't ever show acts of giving up
keep praying and pushing life along
Disabilities may think they are the winner
God's power of healing, will prove them wrong

JUDGING OTHERS

Showing attitude being negative,
judging others by looks or actions
Constant talking of your problems
is not the way of life for Christian

As Christian live with God in heart
and pray for others to love God too
But if others are living in wrong way
God is the one to tell them, not you

Don't allow outer troubles to affect you
give love and kindness to those you meet
And if your talk to others has been wrong
an apology for forgiveness is a treat

Keep thoughts on all goodness received
ignore all bad outside of your heart
Only live for God and his blessings
pushing negative from positive far apart

SPEAK THE TRUTH

When speaking to another
they're hearing words as spoken
Remember those who are listening
are judging your words as a token

So if these words you speak
are not from source of truth
You're falsely drawing people into
a deceitful type of booth

Once your ways are known by others
you will lose trust and all respect
Others will then begin to avoid you
due to being titled as a reject

If you want to remain sociable
and looked at as good in others' eyes
Speak honest and always truthful
and avoid the evilness of telling lies

Coping with Illness

If you have illness in your body
doctors treat as they are taught
For total cure of this illness
God's healing hand must be sought

Medicine is a tested science
God's blessing is a proven heal
With serious illness both are needed receiving
God's curing is best deal

Don't let illness alter your mind
making you feel there's no hope
Tell this evil illness to leave your body
with God in heart you'll be able to cope

Sometimes these illnesses will vanish
some worsening without understand
Just stay positive and pray boldly
your days of life are in God's hands

Move Forward, Never Back

When God chooses saving your life
it's not done without his cause
God's reason being you still to serve
not for putting your life on pause

Service for God will be his choice
always having love and help involved
Listen closely and God will guide you
and provide the talents to evolve

Never waste thoughts on past events
God's blessings always have reasons
Give God praise and move forward
to ignore blessing is form of treason

Disablements from past mean nothing
God will give the strength you need
To accomplish the goals required
knowing God is the power of lead

Never take blessings for granted
God does not give them as a form of waste
Keep moving forward, never move back
God's saving of you gives life new taste

Others' Faults

When something goes wrong for you
not being a fault of yours done
Ones whose failures caused this problem
should not be allowed to turn and run

God above all knows what happened
and all of us will answer for what we do
Don't let another's fault bring you down
God's help will deliver good results for you

Just ask God for the help you need
and whether from a court or insurance
God will guide them towards your way
so you won't suffer for another's ignorance

Again don't put burden on your back
for any wrong not responsible for doing
Believe me, God will correct this for you
and the person at fault will suffer the losing

My Failures

When I shed my tears for
hardships I created with sin
God has forgotten them with forgiveness
and I shall also forget them due to him

It's just so hard to live
with failure in your past
Affecting the woman you love
with your actions made so rash

Wife not holding blame over me
just constantly working for solution
To correct my wrong decisions
the cause of our life's pollution

My faith in God always helps us
giving strength back to us to succeed
The reason I will not repeat my failures
and will put God and my wife to lead

MY THANKSGIVING DAY

Piling a plate so full, with all types of food
holding plate towards nose, food smelling so fresh
Before bite taken, I realized no one had thanked God
and without praise to God, it's like eating plate of mess

Knowing this is not how I was raised, or how I live my life
I said a silent prayer to God, before taking my first bite
Then feeling sense of heaviness, as others sat around
I knew the lack of God's presence in home, just wasn't right

A day named Thanksgiving, to many just a joke
people overeating of food, and getting bellies full
With no thought to the true meaning of this special day
so what, another meal with family and shooting bull

After finishing my meal, I took plate back to kitchen
then went and sat back down, to watch some TV
Grandchildren were playing, others not much talking
did not take long for depression to come over me

All I wanted to do at this point was to get up and leave
at home knowing feeling of God would be back with me
Being with this family of mine, not what I call Thanksgiving
it was just eating a meal, I could say was free

LIFE AND DEATH

Living with God in your heart
walking with Jesus by your side
No worries or fears should you have
when God chooses your time to die

Experiencing the pain and suffering
God knows the amount you stand
The brain has tolerance modes for this
created as a gift from God's healing hands

When the time of passing on greets you
a joyful trip with no thoughts of time
Leading you to a light of comfort
while praising God for peace of mind

Arrival is the ultimate blessing
seeing the line of those in life you loved
Staring down upon you with glowing happiness
inviting your entry into heaven above

God's choice may be to save and return
don't feel your soul has been denied
God is showing he still has a path for you
and will guide you to help others still alive

My Funeral from Above

Yeah, it finally happened to me
heart stopped, and I bit the dust
And hauled down to the funeral home
before my body started to rust

First, that guy pumped my blood out
embalming me with his special stuff
Making me truly look real white
and making my skin look so darn rough

Then put me into costly coffin
leaving head side door wide open
So people could look and sadly say
he's finally gone, what I've been hopen'

Then funeral service was started
all benches full, what's the deal
Probably due to family spreading message
come to this funeral and get a free meal

Well, then they close and seal my lid
hearing someone talking about my life
And where they came up with this about me
certainly didn't come from family or wife

Now all this didn't really matter
because I truly was not in that box
I'm up above looking down on this
just like a sly old fox

Now I'm dropped six feet under
and they covered me up with dirt
But it didn't bother me one darn bit
finally being away from all you squirts

Now blessed and up in heaven
oh, so much better than life on earth
And God's judgment has proven to me
to him my lifestyle wasn't the worst